# 50 Premium World Dinner Recipes for Home

By: Kelly Johnson

# Table of Contents

- Coq au Vin (France)
- Beef Wellington (United Kingdom)
- Pad Thai (Thailand)
- Paella (Spain)
- Chicken Tikka Masala (India)
- Sushi (Japan)
- Ratatouille (France)
- Osso Buco (Italy)
- Moussaka (Greece)
- Ceviche (Peru)
- Jollof Rice (Nigeria)
- Biryani (India)
- Tagine (Morocco)
- Goulash (Hungary)
- Fajitas (Mexico)
- Pho (Vietnam)
- Katsu Curry (Japan)
- Samosas (India)
- Bouillabaisse (France)
- Gnocchi with Pesto (Italy)
- Ramen (Japan)
- Carnitas (Mexico)
- Vindaloo (India)
- Bangers and Mash (United Kingdom)
- Kimchi Jjigae (South Korea)
- Chicken Adobo (Philippines)
- Beef Stroganoff (Russia)
- Borscht (Ukraine)
- Churrasco (Brazil)
- Seafood Paella (Spain)

- Arroz con Pollo (Latin America)
- Chicken Satay (Indonesia)
- Beef Bourguignon (France)
- Ratatouille Tart (France)
- Enchiladas (Mexico)
- Cabbage Rolls (Poland)
- Frikadeller (Denmark)
- Peking Duck (China)
- Italian Sausage and Peppers (Italy)
- Cacio e Pepe (Italy)
- Beef Rendang (Indonesia)
- Dolma (Turkey)
- Kebab (Middle East)
- Laksa (Malaysia)
- Crab Cakes (USA)
- Shakshuka (North Africa)
- Biryani (Pakistan)
- Spanakopita (Greece)
- Maki Rolls (Japan)
- Beef Empanadas (Argentina)

**Osso Buco (Italy)**

Ingredients:

- 4 veal shanks, cut into 1.5-inch pieces
- Salt and pepper to taste
- 1/4 cup all-purpose flour
- 2 tablespoons olive oil
- 1 onion, chopped
- 2 carrots, chopped
- 2 celery stalks, chopped
- 2 garlic cloves, minced
- 1 cup dry white wine
- 1 cup beef or chicken stock
- 1 can (14 oz) diced tomatoes
- 2 sprigs fresh thyme
- 1 bay leaf
- Zest of 1 lemon
- Chopped parsley for garnish

Instructions:

1. Season the veal shanks with salt and pepper, then dust with flour.
2. Heat olive oil in a large pot over medium heat and brown the veal on all sides.
3. Remove the veal and add onion, carrots, celery, and garlic; sauté until softened.
4. Deglaze the pot with white wine, scraping up any browned bits.
5. Add stock, tomatoes, thyme, and bay leaf. Return the veal to the pot, cover, and simmer for 1.5-2 hours, until tender.
6. Serve with lemon zest and chopped parsley on top.

**Moussaka (Greece)**

Ingredients:

- 2 eggplants, sliced
- Salt
- 1 lb ground beef or lamb
- 1 onion, chopped
- 2 garlic cloves, minced
- 1 can (14 oz) diced tomatoes
- 1 teaspoon cinnamon
- 1/2 teaspoon allspice
- 1/4 cup olive oil
- 1/4 cup breadcrumbs
- 2 cups béchamel sauce
- Grated cheese for topping

Instructions:

1. Sprinkle eggplant slices with salt and let sit for 30 minutes; rinse and pat dry.
2. In a skillet, cook the ground meat with onion and garlic until browned. Add tomatoes, cinnamon, and allspice; simmer for 20 minutes.
3. In another skillet, heat olive oil and fry the eggplant slices until golden.
4. In a baking dish, layer half the eggplant, the meat mixture, and the remaining eggplant. Pour béchamel sauce on top and sprinkle with cheese.
5. Bake at 350°F (175°C) for 45 minutes until golden. Let cool before serving.

**Ceviche (Peru)**

Ingredients:

- 1 lb fresh white fish (e.g., tilapia or sea bass), diced
- 1 cup fresh lime juice
- 1 red onion, thinly sliced
- 1-2 jalapeños, minced
- 1 cup chopped cilantro
- Salt to taste
- Avocado slices for serving

Instructions:

1. In a bowl, combine the fish and lime juice; let marinate for 15-20 minutes until the fish is opaque.
2. Add red onion, jalapeños, cilantro, and salt; mix well.
3. Serve chilled with avocado slices on top.

**Jollof Rice (Nigeria)**

Ingredients:

- 2 cups long-grain parboiled rice
- 1/4 cup vegetable oil
- 1 onion, chopped
- 1 bell pepper, chopped
- 2 tomatoes, blended
- 1 tablespoon tomato paste
- 2 cups chicken or vegetable broth
- 1 teaspoon thyme
- 1 teaspoon curry powder
- Salt and pepper to taste

Instructions:

1. Heat oil in a pot; sauté onion and bell pepper until soft.
2. Add blended tomatoes and tomato paste; cook for 10 minutes.
3. Stir in rice, broth, thyme, curry powder, salt, and pepper; bring to a boil.
4. Cover and reduce heat; simmer for 20-25 minutes until rice is cooked and liquid is absorbed.

**Biryani (India)**

Ingredients:

- 2 cups basmati rice
- 1 lb chicken or lamb, cut into pieces
- 1 onion, thinly sliced
- 2 tomatoes, chopped
- 2-3 green chilies, slit
- 1 cup yogurt
- 1/4 cup chopped mint and cilantro
- 1 teaspoon garam masala
- 1/2 teaspoon turmeric
- 4 cups water
- Salt to taste
- Fried onions for garnish

Instructions:

1. Soak the rice for 30 minutes, then drain.
2. In a pot, heat oil and sauté onions until golden. Add meat, tomatoes, chilies, yogurt, mint, cilantro, spices, and salt; cook until meat is browned.
3. Add water and bring to a boil. Add rice, reduce heat, cover, and simmer for 20-25 minutes until rice is cooked.
4. Fluff and garnish with fried onions before serving.

**Tagine (Morocco)**

Ingredients:

- 2 lbs chicken or lamb, cut into pieces
- 1 onion, chopped
- 2 garlic cloves, minced
- 1 teaspoon ground cumin
- 1 teaspoon ground ginger
- 1 teaspoon cinnamon
- 1 can (14 oz) chickpeas, drained
- 2 cups chicken broth
- 1 cup dried apricots
- 1/4 cup almonds
- Fresh cilantro for garnish

Instructions:

1. In a tagine or Dutch oven, heat oil and sauté onions and garlic until soft.
2. Add meat and spices; brown on all sides.
3. Add chickpeas, broth, apricots, and almonds; cover and simmer for 1.5 hours until tender.
4. Garnish with fresh cilantro before serving.

**Goulash (Hungary)**

Ingredients:

- 2 lbs beef chuck, cut into cubes
- 2 onions, chopped
- 2 tablespoons paprika
- 4 garlic cloves, minced
- 4 cups beef broth
- 4 carrots, chopped
- 2 potatoes, cubed
- 1 bell pepper, chopped
- Salt and pepper to taste

Instructions:

1. In a pot, sauté onions until translucent.
2. Add beef and brown on all sides. Stir in paprika and garlic.
3. Pour in beef broth; add carrots, potatoes, bell pepper, salt, and pepper.
4. Simmer for 1.5-2 hours until beef is tender. Serve warm.

Enjoy these flavorful international dishes!

**Osso Buco (Italy)**

Ingredients:

- 4 veal shanks, cut into 1.5-inch pieces
- Salt and pepper to taste
- 1/4 cup all-purpose flour
- 2 tablespoons olive oil
- 1 onion, chopped
- 2 carrots, chopped
- 2 celery stalks, chopped
- 2 garlic cloves, minced
- 1 cup dry white wine
- 1 cup beef or chicken stock
- 1 can (14 oz) diced tomatoes
- 2 sprigs fresh thyme
- 1 bay leaf
- Zest of 1 lemon
- Chopped parsley for garnish

Instructions:

1. Season the veal shanks with salt and pepper, then dust with flour.
2. Heat olive oil in a large pot over medium heat and brown the veal on all sides.
3. Remove the veal and add onion, carrots, celery, and garlic; sauté until softened.
4. Deglaze the pot with white wine, scraping up any browned bits.
5. Add stock, tomatoes, thyme, and bay leaf. Return the veal to the pot, cover, and simmer for 1.5-2 hours, until tender.
6. Serve with lemon zest and chopped parsley on top.

**Moussaka (Greece)**

Ingredients:

- 2 eggplants, sliced
- Salt
- 1 lb ground beef or lamb
- 1 onion, chopped
- 2 garlic cloves, minced
- 1 can (14 oz) diced tomatoes
- 1 teaspoon cinnamon
- 1/2 teaspoon allspice
- 1/4 cup olive oil
- 1/4 cup breadcrumbs
- 2 cups béchamel sauce
- Grated cheese for topping

Instructions:

1. Sprinkle eggplant slices with salt and let sit for 30 minutes; rinse and pat dry.
2. In a skillet, cook the ground meat with onion and garlic until browned. Add tomatoes, cinnamon, and allspice; simmer for 20 minutes.
3. In another skillet, heat olive oil and fry the eggplant slices until golden.
4. In a baking dish, layer half the eggplant, the meat mixture, and the remaining eggplant. Pour béchamel sauce on top and sprinkle with cheese.
5. Bake at 350°F (175°C) for 45 minutes until golden. Let cool before serving.

**Ceviche (Peru)**

Ingredients:

- 1 lb fresh white fish (e.g., tilapia or sea bass), diced
- 1 cup fresh lime juice
- 1 red onion, thinly sliced
- 1-2 jalapeños, minced
- 1 cup chopped cilantro
- Salt to taste
- Avocado slices for serving

Instructions:

1. In a bowl, combine the fish and lime juice; let marinate for 15-20 minutes until the fish is opaque.
2. Add red onion, jalapeños, cilantro, and salt; mix well.
3. Serve chilled with avocado slices on top.

**Jollof Rice (Nigeria)**

Ingredients:

- 2 cups long-grain parboiled rice
- 1/4 cup vegetable oil
- 1 onion, chopped
- 1 bell pepper, chopped
- 2 tomatoes, blended
- 1 tablespoon tomato paste
- 2 cups chicken or vegetable broth
- 1 teaspoon thyme
- 1 teaspoon curry powder
- Salt and pepper to taste

Instructions:

1. Heat oil in a pot; sauté onion and bell pepper until soft.
2. Add blended tomatoes and tomato paste; cook for 10 minutes.
3. Stir in rice, broth, thyme, curry powder, salt, and pepper; bring to a boil.
4. Cover and reduce heat; simmer for 20-25 minutes until rice is cooked and liquid is absorbed.

**Biryani (India)**

Ingredients:

- 2 cups basmati rice
- 1 lb chicken or lamb, cut into pieces
- 1 onion, thinly sliced
- 2 tomatoes, chopped
- 2-3 green chilies, slit
- 1 cup yogurt
- 1/4 cup chopped mint and cilantro
- 1 teaspoon garam masala
- 1/2 teaspoon turmeric
- 4 cups water
- Salt to taste
- Fried onions for garnish

Instructions:

1. Soak the rice for 30 minutes, then drain.
2. In a pot, heat oil and sauté onions until golden. Add meat, tomatoes, chilies, yogurt, mint, cilantro, spices, and salt; cook until meat is browned.
3. Add water and bring to a boil. Add rice, reduce heat, cover, and simmer for 20-25 minutes until rice is cooked.
4. Fluff and garnish with fried onions before serving.

**Tagine (Morocco)**

Ingredients:

- 2 lbs chicken or lamb, cut into pieces
- 1 onion, chopped
- 2 garlic cloves, minced
- 1 teaspoon ground cumin
- 1 teaspoon ground ginger
- 1 teaspoon cinnamon
- 1 can (14 oz) chickpeas, drained
- 2 cups chicken broth
- 1 cup dried apricots
- 1/4 cup almonds
- Fresh cilantro for garnish

Instructions:

1. In a tagine or Dutch oven, heat oil and sauté onions and garlic until soft.
2. Add meat and spices; brown on all sides.
3. Add chickpeas, broth, apricots, and almonds; cover and simmer for 1.5 hours until tender.
4. Garnish with fresh cilantro before serving.

**Goulash (Hungary)**

Ingredients:

- 2 lbs beef chuck, cut into cubes
- 2 onions, chopped
- 2 tablespoons paprika
- 4 garlic cloves, minced
- 4 cups beef broth
- 4 carrots, chopped
- 2 potatoes, cubed
- 1 bell pepper, chopped
- Salt and pepper to taste

Instructions:

1. In a pot, sauté onions until translucent.
2. Add beef and brown on all sides. Stir in paprika and garlic.
3. Pour in beef broth; add carrots, potatoes, bell pepper, salt, and pepper.
4. Simmer for 1.5-2 hours until beef is tender. Serve warm.

Enjoy these flavorful international dishes!

**Fajitas (Mexico)**
**Ingredients:**

- 1 lb flank steak or chicken breast, sliced
- 2 bell peppers, sliced
- 1 onion, sliced
- 2 tablespoons olive oil
- 2 teaspoons chili powder
- 1 teaspoon cumin
- Salt and pepper to taste
- Tortillas for serving
- Optional toppings: sour cream, guacamole, salsa, cheese

**Instructions:**

1. In a bowl, combine olive oil, chili powder, cumin, salt, and pepper. Add the sliced meat and marinate for 30 minutes.
2. Heat a skillet over medium-high heat and cook the marinated meat until browned and cooked through.
3. Remove the meat and add the bell peppers and onion to the same skillet; sauté until tender.
4. Serve the meat and veggies in warm tortillas with desired toppings.

**Pho (Vietnam)**
**Ingredients:**

- 8 cups beef or chicken broth
- 1 lb rice noodles (bánh phở)
- 1 lb beef (e.g., brisket, sirloin), thinly sliced
- 1 onion, sliced
- 2-3 cloves garlic, minced
- 1 piece ginger, sliced
- 1 star anise
- 1 cinnamon stick
- Fresh herbs (basil, cilantro, mint)
- Lime wedges
- Bean sprouts
- Sriracha and hoisin sauce for serving

**Instructions:**

1. In a pot, combine broth, onion, garlic, ginger, star anise, and cinnamon; bring to a simmer. Cook for about 30 minutes.
2. Strain the broth and return it to the pot.
3. Cook rice noodles according to package instructions; drain.
4. To serve, place noodles in a bowl, top with raw beef slices, and ladle hot broth over. Garnish with herbs, lime, and bean sprouts.

**Katsu Curry (Japan)**
**Ingredients:**

- 2 boneless chicken breasts
- Salt and pepper to taste
- 1/2 cup flour
- 1 egg, beaten
- 1 cup panko breadcrumbs
- Vegetable oil for frying
- 1 onion, sliced
- 2 carrots, sliced
- 2 potatoes, cubed
- 4 cups chicken broth
- 1-2 tablespoons curry powder
- Cooked rice for serving

**Instructions:**

1. Season chicken with salt and pepper, then coat in flour, dip in egg, and coat with panko.
2. Heat oil in a pan and fry chicken until golden and cooked through; slice and set aside.
3. In a separate pot, sauté onion, carrots, and potatoes until softened.
4. Add broth and curry powder; simmer until vegetables are tender.
5. Serve the chicken on top of rice, smothered with curry sauce.

**Samosas (India)**
**Ingredients:**

- 2 cups all-purpose flour
- 1/4 cup vegetable oil
- Water (as needed)
- 2 potatoes, boiled and mashed
- 1/2 cup green peas
- 1 teaspoon cumin seeds
- 1 teaspoon garam masala
- Salt to taste
- Oil for deep frying

**Instructions:**

1. In a bowl, mix flour, oil, and salt. Add water gradually to form a dough; knead and let rest.
2. In a pan, heat oil and add cumin seeds; sauté until fragrant. Add peas and mashed potatoes, garam masala, and salt; mix well.
3. Roll out dough into circles, cut in half, and form a cone. Fill with potato mixture, seal, and deep fry until golden.

**Bouillabaisse (France)**
**Ingredients:**

- 2 tablespoons olive oil
- 1 onion, chopped
- 2 garlic cloves, minced
- 1 leeks, sliced
- 1 can (14 oz) diced tomatoes
- 4 cups fish stock
- 1 teaspoon saffron threads
- 1 lb mixed fish (e.g., cod, mussels, shrimp)
- 1/2 cup white wine
- Salt and pepper to taste
- Fresh parsley for garnish

**Instructions:**

1. In a large pot, heat olive oil; sauté onion, garlic, and leeks until soft.
2. Add tomatoes, fish stock, saffron, and wine; bring to a simmer.
3. Add the fish and cook until tender. Season with salt and pepper.
4. Serve hot, garnished with parsley and crusty bread on the side.

**Gnocchi with Pesto (Italy)**
**Ingredients:**

- 1 lb potato gnocchi
- 1 cup basil pesto (store-bought or homemade)
- 1/4 cup grated Parmesan cheese
- Salt to taste
- Cherry tomatoes (optional)

**Instructions:**

1. Cook gnocchi in salted boiling water until they float; drain.
2. In a pan, combine cooked gnocchi with pesto and heat through.
3. Serve topped with Parmesan cheese and halved cherry tomatoes, if desired.

**Ramen (Japan)**
**Ingredients:**

- 4 cups chicken or vegetable broth
- 2 packs ramen noodles
- 1 cup sliced mushrooms
- 2 green onions, chopped
- 2 eggs
- Soy sauce to taste
- Nori (seaweed) for garnish

**Instructions:**

1. In a pot, bring broth to a simmer and add mushrooms and green onions.
2. Cook ramen noodles according to package instructions and add to the broth.
3. Boil eggs until soft-boiled, peel, and halve.
4. Serve ramen in bowls, topped with eggs and nori. Add soy sauce to taste.

Enjoy these delicious international dishes!

# Carnitas

## Ingredients:

- 3-4 lbs pork shoulder (also called pork butt), cut into large chunks
- 1 onion, quartered
- 4 cloves garlic, minced
- 1 orange, juiced (and keep the spent halves)
- 1 lime, juiced
- 1 tsp cumin
- 1 tsp oregano
- 1 tsp salt
- ½ tsp black pepper
- ½ tsp chili powder (optional for heat)
- 1 cup chicken broth or water
- Bay leaves (2-3)
- Lard or vegetable oil (for frying)

Instructions:

1. Prepare the Pork:
   - Place the pork shoulder chunks in a large slow cooker or Dutch oven. Add the quartered onion, minced garlic, orange juice, lime juice, cumin, oregano, salt, black pepper, and chili powder. Toss to combine.
   - Squeeze the juice from the spent orange halves into the pot and then place the halves in with the meat.
2. Cook the Pork:
   - Pour the chicken broth or water over the pork and add the bay leaves. Cover and cook on low for about 8 hours or on high for 4 hours, until the pork is tender and shreds easily with a fork.
3. Shred the Meat:
   - Once cooked, remove the pork from the pot and shred it using two forks. Discard any large pieces of fat and the bay leaves. Reserve some of the cooking liquid.
4. Crisp the Carnitas:
   - In a large skillet, heat a couple of tablespoons of lard or vegetable oil over medium-high heat. Add the shredded pork in batches, pressing it down into the skillet to form a crispy layer. Fry for about 4-5 minutes until the

edges are crispy and golden brown. If needed, add a bit of the reserved cooking liquid to keep the meat moist.
   5. Serve:
      - Serve the carnitas with warm tortillas, cilantro, diced onions, lime wedges, and your favorite toppings like salsa or guacamole.

Tips:

- For added flavor, you can include spices like cinnamon or cloves in the slow cooker.
- Cooking in batches helps achieve a crispy texture, as overcrowding the pan can cause the meat to steam rather than crisp.
- Leftover carnitas can be stored in an airtight container in the refrigerator for up to 3 days or frozen for longer storage.

Enjoy your delicious homemade carnitas!

## Vindaloo (India)

**Ingredients:**

- 2 lbs pork shoulder, cut into cubes
- 2 onions, finely chopped
- 4 cloves garlic, minced
- 1-inch piece ginger, minced
- 2-3 green chilies, chopped
- 2 tbsp vinegar (preferably malt vinegar)
- 1 tsp turmeric powder
- 1 tsp cumin seeds
- 1 tsp mustard seeds
- 1 tsp black peppercorns
- 2-3 dried red chilies
- 1 tsp cinnamon powder
- 1 tbsp sugar
- Salt to taste
- 3-4 tbsp oil

Instructions:

1. Marinate the Pork: In a bowl, combine pork cubes with vinegar, turmeric, and salt. Let it marinate for at least 1 hour.
2. Make the Spice Paste: In a dry pan, roast cumin seeds, mustard seeds, black peppercorns, and dried red chilies until fragrant. Grind into a paste with garlic, ginger, and green chilies.
3. Cook the Onions: Heat oil in a pot. Add chopped onions and sauté until golden brown.
4. Add Spices: Stir in the spice paste and cook for a few minutes. Add sugar and cinnamon.
5. Add Pork: Add the marinated pork and cook until browned. Pour in water to cover the meat and simmer until tender.
6. Serve: Adjust salt and serve hot with rice or bread.

## Bangers and Mash (United Kingdom)

Ingredients:

- 8 pork sausages (your choice)
- 2 lbs potatoes, peeled and chopped
- 1 cup milk
- 4 tbsp butter
- Salt and pepper to taste
- 1 onion, finely sliced
- 2 cups beef or onion gravy

Instructions:

1. Cook the Sausages: Grill or pan-fry sausages until cooked through. Set aside.
2. Prepare the Mash: Boil potatoes in salted water until tender. Drain and mash with milk, butter, salt, and pepper.
3. Cook the Onions: In the same pan, sauté onions until golden.
4. Serve: Plate the mashed potatoes, top with sausages, and pour gravy over everything.

## Kimchi Jjigae (South Korea)

Ingredients:

- 1 cup kimchi, chopped
- 1 lb pork belly or tofu, cut into cubes
- 1 onion, sliced
- 2 green onions, chopped
- 2 cups water or broth
- 1 tbsp gochugaru (Korean chili flakes)
- 1 tbsp soy sauce
- 1 tsp sesame oil
- Optional: tofu, mushrooms, or other vegetables

Instructions:

1. Cook the Meat: In a pot, cook the pork belly until browned. If using tofu, add later.
2. Add Kimchi: Stir in chopped kimchi and cook for a few minutes.
3. Add Liquids: Pour in water or broth, add gochugaru, soy sauce, and sesame oil. Bring to a boil.
4. Simmer: Reduce heat and simmer for about 20 minutes. Add tofu and other vegetables if desired.
5. Serve: Garnish with green onions and serve hot with rice.

## Chicken Adobo (Philippines)

Ingredients:

- 2 lbs chicken, cut into pieces
- 1/2 cup soy sauce
- 1/2 cup vinegar (cane vinegar preferred)
- 1 onion, sliced
- 4 cloves garlic, minced
- 2-3 bay leaves
- 1 tsp black peppercorns
- 1-2 tbsp sugar (optional)
- 2 tbsp oil

Instructions:

1. Marinate Chicken: In a bowl, combine chicken, soy sauce, vinegar, garlic, onion, bay leaves, and peppercorns. Marinate for at least 30 minutes.
2. Cook the Chicken: Heat oil in a pot. Add marinated chicken and cook until browned.
3. Simmer: Pour in the marinade, add sugar if using, and simmer for about 30 minutes until chicken is tender.
4. Serve: Serve hot with rice.

## Beef Stroganoff (Russia)

Ingredients:

- 1 lb beef sirloin, thinly sliced
- 1 onion, chopped
- 2 cups mushrooms, sliced
- 2 cloves garlic, minced
- 1 cup beef broth
- 1 cup sour cream
- 2 tbsp flour
- 2 tbsp butter
- Salt and pepper to taste
- Egg noodles or rice for serving

Instructions:

1. Sauté Beef: In a skillet, melt butter and sauté beef until browned. Remove and set aside.
2. Cook Onions and Mushrooms: In the same skillet, add onions and mushrooms, cooking until soft. Add garlic and cook for another minute.
3. Make Sauce: Sprinkle flour over the mixture, stir, then gradually add beef broth. Bring to a simmer.
4. Combine: Return beef to the skillet, stir in sour cream, and season with salt and pepper. Heat through.
5. Serve: Serve over cooked egg noodles or rice.

## Borscht (Ukraine)

Ingredients:

- 2 beets, peeled and grated
- 1 onion, chopped
- 1 carrot, grated
- 1 potato, diced
- 1/2 cabbage, shredded
- 1-2 cloves garlic, minced
- 6 cups vegetable or beef broth
- 2 tbsp tomato paste
- 1 tbsp vinegar (optional)
- Salt and pepper to taste
- Fresh dill or parsley for garnish
- Sour cream for serving

Instructions:

1. Sauté Vegetables: In a large pot, sauté onions, carrots, and beets until softened.
2. Add Broth: Pour in the broth and add potatoes, cabbage, and tomato paste. Bring to a boil.
3. Simmer: Reduce heat and simmer for about 30-40 minutes until vegetables are tender. Add vinegar, salt, and pepper to taste.
4. Serve: Ladle into bowls and garnish with fresh dill or parsley. Serve with sour cream.

## Churrasco (Brazil)

Ingredients:

- 2 lbs beef (such as flank steak or sirloin)
- 2 cloves garlic, minced
- 1/4 cup olive oil
- 1 tbsp salt
- 1 tsp black pepper
- 1 tbsp fresh herbs (parsley or cilantro, chopped)
- Lemon wedges for serving

Instructions:

1. Marinate the Meat: In a bowl, mix garlic, olive oil, salt, pepper, and herbs. Coat the beef with the marinade and let it rest for at least 30 minutes.
2. Grill the Beef: Preheat the grill to medium-high heat. Grill the beef for about 5-7 minutes on each side or until cooked to your liking.
3. Rest and Slice: Remove from the grill and let the meat rest for a few minutes before slicing against the grain.
4. Serve: Serve with lemon wedges on the side.

## Seafood Paella (Spain)

Ingredients:

- 2 cups Bomba or Arborio rice
- 4 cups seafood broth
- 1 onion, chopped
- 4 cloves garlic, minced
- 1 bell pepper, chopped
- 1 cup diced tomatoes (canned or fresh)
- 1/2 cup peas (optional)
- 1 lb mixed seafood (shrimp, mussels, squid)
- 1 tsp smoked paprika
- 1/4 tsp saffron threads (optional)
- Salt and pepper to taste
- Olive oil for cooking
- Fresh parsley for garnish
- Lemon wedges for serving

Instructions:

1. Sauté Vegetables: In a large paella pan or skillet, heat olive oil and sauté onion, garlic, and bell pepper until softened.
2. Add Rice and Broth: Stir in the rice, diced tomatoes, smoked paprika, and saffron. Pour in the seafood broth and bring to a boil.
3. Cook Seafood: Reduce heat and simmer for about 10-15 minutes without stirring. Add mixed seafood and peas. Cook until seafood is cooked through and rice is tender, about 10 more minutes.
4. Serve: Garnish with fresh parsley and serve with lemon wedges.

## Arroz con Pollo (Latin America)

Ingredients:

- 2 lbs chicken (legs, thighs, or breasts)
- 2 cups rice
- 1 onion, chopped
- 2 cloves garlic, minced
- 1 bell pepper, chopped
- 1 can (14 oz) diced tomatoes
- 4 cups chicken broth
- 1 tsp cumin
- 1 tsp paprika
- Salt and pepper to taste
- 1/2 cup peas (optional)
- Olive oil for cooking
- Fresh cilantro for garnish

Instructions:

1. Brown the Chicken: In a large pot, heat olive oil and brown the chicken pieces. Remove and set aside.
2. Sauté Vegetables: In the same pot, sauté onion, garlic, and bell pepper until softened.
3. Add Rice and Broth: Stir in rice, tomatoes, cumin, paprika, and return the chicken to the pot. Pour in chicken broth and bring to a boil.
4. Simmer: Reduce heat, cover, and simmer for about 20-25 minutes until rice is cooked. Add peas if using and cook for an additional 5 minutes.
5. Serve: Garnish with fresh cilantro and serve hot.

## Chicken Satay (Indonesia)

Ingredients:

- 1 lb chicken breast, cut into strips
- 2 tbsp soy sauce
- 2 tbsp peanut butter
- 1 tbsp honey
- 1 tbsp lime juice
- 2 cloves garlic, minced
- 1 tsp ground coriander
- Salt and pepper to taste
- Skewers (soaked in water if wooden)

Instructions:

1. Marinate Chicken: In a bowl, combine soy sauce, peanut butter, honey, lime juice, garlic, coriander, salt, and pepper. Add chicken strips and marinate for at least 30 minutes.
2. Prepare Skewers: Thread chicken strips onto skewers.
3. Grill: Preheat the grill to medium-high heat. Grill skewers for about 5-7 minutes on each side until cooked through.
4. Serve: Serve with peanut sauce and cucumber salad.

## Beef Bourguignon (France)

Ingredients:

- 2 lbs beef chuck, cut into cubes
- 1 bottle (750 ml) red wine (preferably Burgundy)
- 2 cups beef broth
- 4 oz bacon, diced
- 1 onion, chopped
- 2 carrots, sliced
- 4 cloves garlic, minced
- 2 tbsp flour
- 1 bouquet garni (herbs like thyme, bay leaf)
- Salt and pepper to taste
- 2 tbsp olive oil
- 1 cup pearl onions (optional)
- 1 cup mushrooms, sliced

Instructions:

1. Brown the Bacon: In a large Dutch oven, cook bacon until crispy. Remove and set aside.
2. Brown the Beef: In the same pot, add olive oil and brown the beef in batches. Remove and set aside.
3. Sauté Vegetables: Add onion, carrots, and garlic to the pot and sauté until softened.
4. Add Flour and Liquid: Sprinkle flour over the vegetables, stir, and cook for a minute. Add red wine and broth, scraping the bottom of the pot.
5. Combine and Simmer: Return beef and bacon to the pot along with the bouquet garni. Bring to a boil, reduce heat, and simmer for 2-3 hours until tender. Add pearl onions and mushrooms in the last 30 minutes.
6. Serve: Serve hot with crusty bread or mashed potatoes.

## Ratatouille Tart (France)

Ingredients:

- 1 pre-made pie crust (store-bought or homemade)
- 1 eggplant, sliced thin
- 1 zucchini, sliced thin
- 1 bell pepper, sliced thin
- 1 onion, sliced thin
- 2-3 tomatoes, sliced thin
- 2 cloves garlic, minced
- 1/4 cup olive oil
- 1 tsp dried thyme
- Salt and pepper to taste
- 1/2 cup grated cheese (like Gruyère or mozzarella)
- Fresh basil for garnish

Instructions:

1. Preheat Oven: Preheat your oven to 400°F (200°C).
2. Prepare Vegetables: In a bowl, toss eggplant, zucchini, bell pepper, and onion with olive oil, garlic, thyme, salt, and pepper.
3. Blind Bake the Crust: Place the pie crust in a tart pan and blind bake for about 10-15 minutes until slightly golden.
4. Assemble Tart: Layer the sliced tomatoes and marinated vegetables in the tart crust. Sprinkle cheese on top.
5. Bake: Bake for 25-30 minutes until vegetables are tender and cheese is bubbly.
6. Serve: Garnish with fresh basil and serve warm or at room temperature.

## Enchiladas (Mexico)

Ingredients:

- 12 corn tortillas
- 2 cups cooked shredded chicken (or beef)
- 2 cups red or green enchilada sauce
- 1 cup shredded cheese (cheddar or Mexican blend)
- 1 onion, chopped
- 1 tsp ground cumin
- 1 tsp garlic powder
- Salt and pepper to taste
- Fresh cilantro for garnish
- Sour cream for serving (optional)

Instructions:

1. Preheat Oven: Preheat your oven to 375°F (190°C).
2. Prepare Filling: In a bowl, mix cooked chicken, chopped onion, cumin, garlic powder, salt, and pepper.
3. Warm Tortillas: Lightly heat tortillas in a dry skillet or microwave until pliable.
4. Fill Tortillas: Spoon some filling into each tortilla, roll it up, and place seam-side down in a baking dish.
5. Add Sauce and Cheese: Pour enchilada sauce over the rolled tortillas and sprinkle cheese on top.
6. Bake: Bake for 20-25 minutes until heated through and cheese is melted.
7. Serve: Garnish with fresh cilantro and serve with sour cream if desired.

## Cabbage Rolls (Poland)

Ingredients:

- 1 large head of cabbage
- 1 lb ground meat (beef, pork, or a mix)
- 1 cup cooked rice
- 1 onion, chopped
- 2 cloves garlic, minced
- 1 can (15 oz) tomato sauce
- 1 tsp paprika
- Salt and pepper to taste
- Fresh dill for garnish

Instructions:

1. Prepare Cabbage: Bring a large pot of water to a boil. Carefully remove cabbage leaves and blanch them for about 2 minutes until softened. Set aside to cool.
2. Make Filling: In a bowl, combine ground meat, cooked rice, onion, garlic, paprika, salt, and pepper.
3. Roll Cabbage: Place about 2 tablespoons of filling in the center of each cabbage leaf, fold in sides, and roll up tightly.
4. Arrange in Pot: Place rolled cabbage in a large pot, seam-side down. Pour tomato sauce over the top.
5. Simmer: Cover and simmer on low heat for about 1-1.5 hours until cooked through.
6. Serve: Garnish with fresh dill and serve hot.

## Frikadeller (Denmark)

Ingredients:

- 1 lb ground beef (or a mix of beef and pork)
- 1/2 cup breadcrumbs
- 1/2 cup milk
- 1 onion, grated
- 1 egg
- Salt and pepper to taste
- Butter for frying

Instructions:

1. Make Mixture: In a bowl, soak breadcrumbs in milk. Add ground meat, grated onion, egg, salt, and pepper. Mix well until combined.
2. Shape Patties: Form mixture into small patties or balls.
3. Fry Patties: In a skillet, heat butter over medium heat. Fry patties for about 5-7 minutes on each side until golden brown and cooked through.
4. Serve: Serve with boiled potatoes and gravy or with a side salad.

## Peking Duck (China)

Ingredients:

- 1 whole duck (about 5-6 lbs)
- 1/4 cup maltose (or honey)
- 1/4 cup soy sauce
- 1 tbsp rice vinegar
- 5-6 slices of ginger
- 3-4 green onions
- Hoisin sauce for serving
- Chinese pancakes or tortillas for wrapping

Instructions:

1. Prepare the Duck: Rinse the duck inside and out, then pat it dry. Use a needle to prick the skin all over (avoid piercing the meat).
2. Marinate: In a bowl, mix maltose, soy sauce, and rice vinegar. Brush the mixture over the duck and let it marinate in the refrigerator for at least 4 hours or overnight.
3. Roast the Duck: Preheat the oven to 375°F (190°C). Place duck on a rack in a roasting pan. Roast for about 1.5 hours, basting occasionally until the skin is crispy and golden.
4. Rest and Serve: Let the duck rest for 15 minutes before carving. Serve with hoisin sauce, sliced ginger, green onions, and pancakes.

## Italian Sausage and Peppers (Italy)

Ingredients:

- 1 lb Italian sausage (sweet or spicy)
- 1 bell pepper (red or yellow), sliced
- 1 onion, sliced
- 2 cloves garlic, minced
- 1 can (14 oz) diced tomatoes
- Olive oil for cooking
- Salt and pepper to taste
- Fresh basil for garnish (optional)

Instructions:

1. Cook Sausage: In a large skillet, heat olive oil over medium heat. Add sausages and cook until browned on all sides. Remove and slice into pieces.
2. Sauté Vegetables: In the same skillet, add sliced bell pepper, onion, and garlic. Sauté until softened.
3. Combine Ingredients: Return sausage to the skillet. Add diced tomatoes, salt, and pepper. Simmer for about 10 minutes.
4. Serve: Garnish with fresh basil if desired. Serve hot with crusty bread or over pasta.

## Cacio e Pepe (Italy)

Ingredients:

- 12 oz spaghetti or tonnarelli
- 1 cup grated Pecorino Romano cheese
- Freshly cracked black pepper
- Salt for pasta water
- 1-2 tbsp pasta cooking water (as needed)

Instructions:

1. Cook Pasta: Bring a large pot of salted water to a boil. Add pasta and cook until al dente. Reserve 1 cup of pasta water before draining.
2. Prepare Sauce: In a large bowl, combine grated Pecorino Romano and a generous amount of black pepper.
3. Mix Pasta and Cheese: Add drained pasta to the bowl with cheese. Pour in a little reserved pasta water, stirring quickly to create a creamy sauce.
4. Serve: Adjust consistency with more pasta water if needed. Serve immediately with extra cheese and pepper on top.

## Beef Rendang (Indonesia)

Ingredients:

- 2 lbs beef (chuck or brisket), cut into cubes
- 1 can (14 oz) coconut milk
- 1 onion, chopped
- 4 cloves garlic, minced
- 2-inch piece ginger, minced
- 2-3 red chilies (or to taste)
- 1 tsp turmeric powder
- 1 tsp cumin powder
- 1 tsp coriander powder
- 1-2 tbsp tamarind paste
- Salt to taste
- 2-3 kaffir lime leaves (optional)

Instructions:

1. Blend Spices: In a blender, combine onion, garlic, ginger, red chilies, turmeric, cumin, and coriander. Blend into a paste.
2. Cook Beef: In a large pot, heat a bit of oil and add the spice paste. Cook for a few minutes until fragrant. Add beef and cook until browned.
3. Add Coconut Milk: Pour in coconut milk and tamarind paste. Stir to combine, then add kaffir lime leaves if using.
4. Simmer: Reduce heat and simmer for about 2-3 hours until beef is tender and sauce thickens. Stir occasionally and add water if necessary to prevent burning.
5. Serve: Serve hot with rice.

# Dolma (Turkey)

Ingredients:

- 1 lb grape leaves (jarred or fresh)
- 1 cup rice
- 1 onion, chopped
- 1/2 cup pine nuts
- 1/2 cup currants or raisins
- 1/2 cup fresh parsley, chopped
- 1/4 cup fresh dill, chopped
- 1/4 cup olive oil
- 1 lemon, juiced
- Salt and pepper to taste
- 2 cups vegetable or chicken broth

Instructions:

1. Prepare Grape Leaves: If using jarred grape leaves, rinse and soak them in hot water for 10 minutes to soften. If using fresh, blanch in boiling water for 2-3 minutes and then cool.
2. Make Filling: In a skillet, heat olive oil over medium heat. Sauté onion until translucent. Add rice, pine nuts, currants, parsley, dill, salt, and pepper. Stir for 2-3 minutes, then add 1 cup of broth. Cook until rice is partially cooked, about 10 minutes. Let cool.
3. Fill Leaves: Lay a grape leaf vein-side up. Place a tablespoon of filling near the stem end, fold in the sides, and roll tightly.
4. Cook Dolmas: Arrange stuffed leaves in a pot, seam-side down. Pour remaining broth and lemon juice over them. Place a plate on top to keep them submerged. Cover and simmer for about 30-40 minutes.
5. Serve: Allow to cool slightly before serving. Serve with yogurt or a drizzle of olive oil.

## Kebab (Middle East)

Ingredients:

- 1 lb ground lamb or beef
- 1 onion, grated
- 2 cloves garlic, minced
- 1 tsp cumin
- 1 tsp coriander
- 1/2 tsp paprika
- Salt and pepper to taste
- Skewers (soaked in water if wooden)

Instructions:

1. Prepare Mixture: In a bowl, combine ground meat, grated onion, garlic, cumin, coriander, paprika, salt, and pepper. Mix well until combined.
2. Shape Kebabs: Divide the mixture into portions and shape them onto skewers.
3. Grill Kebabs: Preheat a grill or grill pan. Cook kebabs over medium-high heat for about 10-12 minutes, turning occasionally until cooked through.
4. Serve: Serve with pita bread, fresh vegetables, and your choice of sauces (e.g., tahini or yogurt sauce).

## Laksa (Malaysia)

Ingredients:

- 200g rice noodles
- 1 lb shrimp or chicken
- 2 cups coconut milk
- 2 cups chicken or vegetable broth
- 2 tbsp laksa paste
- 1/2 cup bean sprouts
- 2 boiled eggs, halved
- Fresh cilantro for garnish
- Lime wedges for serving

Instructions:

1. Cook Noodles: Prepare rice noodles according to package instructions. Drain and set aside.
2. Make Soup Base: In a pot, heat laksa paste over medium heat for a minute. Add chicken or shrimp and cook until browned.
3. Add Liquids: Pour in coconut milk and broth, bring to a simmer, and cook until chicken is done or shrimp is pink.
4. Assemble Bowls: Divide noodles among bowls, ladle the laksa soup over them, and top with bean sprouts and halved eggs.
5. Serve: Garnish with cilantro and serve with lime wedges.

## Crab Cakes (USA)

Ingredients:

- 1 lb crab meat (fresh or canned)
- 1/2 cup breadcrumbs
- 1/4 cup mayonnaise
- 1 egg
- 1 tbsp Dijon mustard
- 1 tbsp Worcestershire sauce
- 1 tsp Old Bay seasoning
- Salt and pepper to taste
- Butter or oil for frying

Instructions:

1. Mix Ingredients: In a bowl, combine crab meat, breadcrumbs, mayonnaise, egg, Dijon mustard, Worcestershire sauce, Old Bay seasoning, salt, and pepper. Mix gently to avoid breaking the crab meat.
2. Form Cakes: Shape the mixture into patties and refrigerate for at least 30 minutes to firm up.
3. Fry Cakes: In a skillet, heat butter or oil over medium heat. Fry crab cakes for about 4-5 minutes on each side until golden brown.
4. Serve: Serve hot with tartar sauce or lemon wedges.

## Shakshuka (North Africa)

Ingredients:

- 4 large eggs
- 1 can (14 oz) diced tomatoes
- 1 onion, chopped
- 1 bell pepper, chopped
- 2 cloves garlic, minced
- 1 tsp ground cumin
- 1 tsp paprika
- Salt and pepper to taste
- Olive oil for cooking
- Fresh parsley for garnish

Instructions:

1. Sauté Vegetables: In a skillet, heat olive oil over medium heat. Add onion and bell pepper, sauté until softened. Stir in garlic, cumin, paprika, salt, and pepper.
2. Add Tomatoes: Pour in diced tomatoes and simmer for about 10 minutes until the sauce thickens.
3. Add Eggs: Create small wells in the sauce and crack an egg into each well. Cover and cook until eggs are set to your liking (about 5-7 minutes).
4. Serve: Garnish with fresh parsley and serve with crusty bread.

# Biryani (Pakistan)

Ingredients:

- 2 cups basmati rice
- 1 lb chicken or beef, cut into pieces
- 1 onion, sliced
- 2 tomatoes, chopped
- 1 cup plain yogurt
- 2 tbsp biryani spice mix
- 2 cups water
- Fresh cilantro and mint for garnish
- Salt to taste
- Oil for cooking

Instructions:

1. Cook Rice: Rinse basmati rice until the water runs clear. Soak for 30 minutes. Cook in salted boiling water until 70% done. Drain and set aside.
2. Sauté Meat: In a large pot, heat oil and sauté sliced onion until golden. Add chicken or beef and cook until browned.
3. Add Tomatoes and Spices: Stir in chopped tomatoes, yogurt, biryani spice mix, and salt. Cook for 5-7 minutes until the meat is cooked through.
4. Layer Biryani: Layer partially cooked rice over the meat mixture. Pour in 2 cups of water. Cover tightly and cook on low heat for 25-30 minutes until rice is fully cooked.
5. Serve: Garnish with fresh cilantro and mint before serving.

## Spanakopita (Greece)

Ingredients:

- 1 lb phyllo dough
- 1 lb spinach, chopped
- 1 cup feta cheese, crumbled
- 1 onion, chopped
- 2 eggs, beaten
- 1/4 cup olive oil
- Salt and pepper to taste
- Fresh dill for flavor (optional)

Instructions:

1. Sauté Spinach: In a skillet, heat olive oil over medium heat. Add onion and cook until translucent. Add spinach and cook until wilted. Allow to cool.
2. Mix Filling: In a bowl, combine spinach mixture, feta cheese, beaten eggs, salt, pepper, and dill (if using).
3. Assemble Phyllo: Preheat oven to 375°F (190°C). Layer several sheets of phyllo in a greased baking dish, brushing each layer with olive oil.
4. Fill and Fold: Spoon the filling onto the phyllo and fold the edges over. Layer more phyllo sheets on top, brushing with olive oil.
5. Bake: Bake for 30-40 minutes until golden brown. Allow to cool slightly before slicing and serving.

## Maki Rolls (Japan)

Ingredients:

- 2 cups sushi rice
- 1/4 cup rice vinegar
- 1 tbsp sugar
- 1/2 tsp salt
- Nori sheets (seaweed)
- Fillings (e.g., cucumber, avocado, crab, or fish)
- Soy sauce for serving
- Wasabi and pickled ginger (optional)

Instructions:

1. Cook Sushi Rice: Rinse sushi rice until water runs clear. Cook rice according to package instructions. Once cooked, mix rice vinegar, sugar, and salt in a bowl and fold into the rice.
2. Prepare Fillings: Slice desired fillings into thin strips.
3. Assemble Rolls: Place a sheet of nori on a bamboo mat. Spread a thin layer of rice over nori, leaving a 1-inch border at the top. Place fillings in a line across the center of the rice.
4. Roll: Roll the bamboo mat tightly away from you, pressing gently to shape the roll. Seal the edge with a little water.
5. Slice and Serve: Use a sharp knife to slice the roll into bite-sized pieces. Serve with soy sauce, wasabi, and pickled ginger.

www.ingramcontent.com/pod-product-compliance
Lightning Source LLC
LaVergne TN
LVHW081501060526
838201LV00056BA/2874